REDBACK publishing

AUSTRALIAN TRANSPORT

SEA TRANSPORT

ALISON HIDEKI

First Published 2018 by
Redback Publishing
Suite 6, 13a Narabang Way,
Belrose NSW 2085
Australia

www.redbackpublishing.com
orders@redbackpublishing.com

ISBN 978-1-761401-58-9

Author: Alison Hideki
Editor: Marianne Lindsell
Designer: Redback Publishing

Original illustrations © Redback Publishing 2025
Originated by Redback Publishing

Acknowledgements
Abbreviations: l—left, r—right, b—bottom, t—top, c—centre, m—middle
We would like to thank the following for permission to reproduce photographs: (Images © shutterstock) p8b Unidentified sailing ship 1900 State Library of Victoria, p9m Kapunda steam ship Allan C. Green via Wikimedia Commons, p12b Scene of the Loss of the Emigrant Ship 'Cataraqui' August 1845, Museums Victoria, p13t Museums Victoria 1962404, p23t The Rip map By Nick carson via Wikipedia, p23b View from below Point Lonsdale Lighthouse, past the jetty, across the Rip towards Point Nepean, Victoria, Australia. By Maias via Wikimedia Commons.

A catalogue record for this book is available from the National Library of Australia

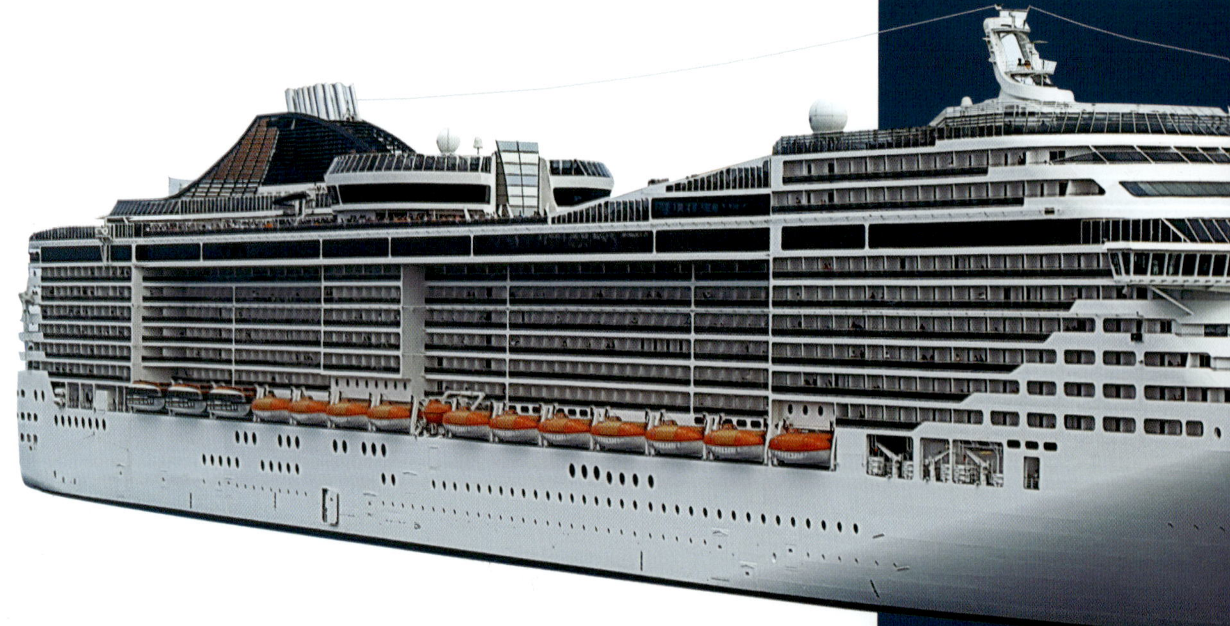

CONTENTS

ABOARD SHIPS

Ships have been an important form of transport for Australia ever since the first European sailing ships began to chart our shores. Smaller sea-going vessels were important to many coastal-living Aboriginal groups long before Europeans brought their ships to Australia.

Today, ships continue to be the main form of transport for international freight.

TRANSPORT

Transport is the movement of people or goods from one place to another. There are many kinds of transport, including airplanes, cars, trucks, ships, trains, pipelines and conveyor belts. Transport has always been very important for humans, as it makes it possible for people to communicate with one another, and to trade with one another.

FREIGHT TRANSPORT

Most goods brought to Australia from overseas travel aboard ships. Many of the cars we travel in, the foods we eat and the electrical goods, such as computers, we use every day were brought to Australia aboard ships. Most goods sold to overseas countries such as coal, iron ore, wool and beef are also transported by ship.

PASSENGER SHIPS

Ships also transport passengers. Until the 1970s they provided the main form of international travel for Australians. Today, the Spirit of Tasmania forms an important passenger transport link between Tasmania and Victoria, and passenger ships still cruise the world providing luxury holidays.

Smaller ships and boats operate between the mainland and other islands, on waterways such as Sydney Harbour and along rivers such as the Murray.

ABORIGINAL BOATS

Many Aboriginal groups living on the coast or near rivers made boats. The most common material used was bark, which was cut from a tree in a large sheet and bound tightly at each end. Other types of boats included rafts made from bark and small logs, and canoes made by hollowing out large logs. In northern Queensland some Aboriginal people made sail-powered outrigger canoes.

POWERING SHIPS

Most modern ships are powered by diesel engines. Small ships have one propeller; large ships have two propellers; and some very large ships have four. The engines make the propellers turn. The turning propellers push water behind the ship to make it move forwards.

EARLY VISITORS

Aboriginal people lived in Australia for thousands of years before the Europeans arrived, and there were occasional visitors from other parts of the world. Chinese and Malay seafarers may have visited during the 1400s. From the 1600s until the early 1900s Indonesians visited Northern Australia in *praus* (sailing boats) each year to gather *trepang* (sea slugs, which were dried for food). People from New Guinea also visited the Torres Strait islands and Cape York, and Aboriginal people travelled by boat to New Guinea and Macassa (in Indonesia).

THE FIRST SEA VOYAGES TO AUSTRALIA

The history of sea travel in Australia began when the first humans arrived more than 50,000 years ago. They probably came from the islands that now form Indonesia, travelling by boat. No one knows exactly how the first journey was achieved. Archaeologists think that they used rafts made of logs lashed together, probably powered by some sort of sail.

THE SPANISH AND THE DUTCH

The first Europeans to visit Australia came aboard sailing ships. In the 1400s, Europeans built ships that could travel long distances over the ocean. During the 1500s and 1600s, they explored the southern Atlantic Ocean, the Indian Ocean and the Pacific Ocean. In 1606, the Spanish sailor Luis Baez de Torres sailed through Torres Strait between New Guinea and Cape York. A few months later, Dutchman Willem Jansz, in a small sailing ship called the Duyfken ('Little Dove'), landed on the western coast of Cape York.

The Duyfken (replica), captained by Willem Jansz, was one of the first European ships to land on Australian shores.

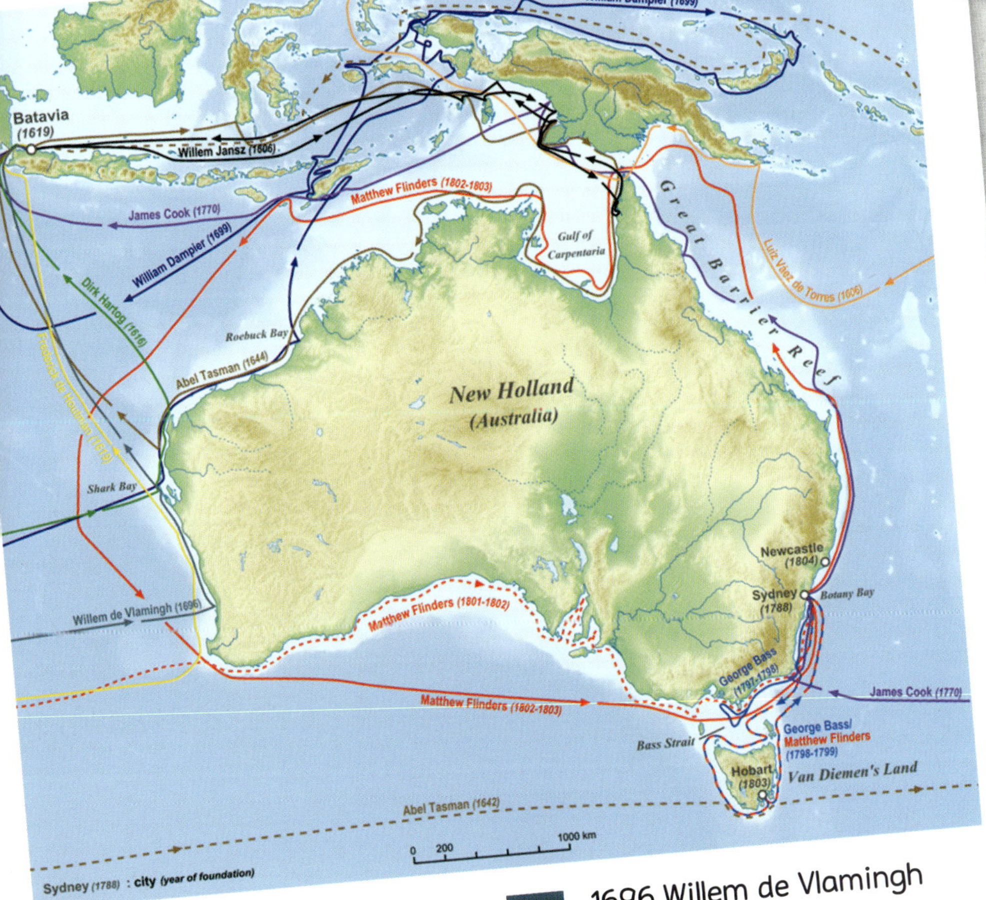

1606 Willem Jansz
1606 Luís Vaz de Torres
1616 Dirk Hartog
1619 Frederick de Houtman
1644 Abel Tasman
1696 Willem de Vlamingh
1699 William Dampier
1770 James Cook
1797-1799 George Bass
1801-1803 Matthew Flinders

THE BRITISH

In 1788, eleven British sailing ships arrived at Botany Bay to begin the European occupation of Australia. The ships carried about 1,000 people, including more than 700 convicts. Captain Arthur Phillip chose Sydney Cove in nearby Port Jackson (Sydney Harbour) to start the settlement. One of the reasons Sydney Cove was chosen was that the water of the cove was deep enough for the ships to be unloaded close to shore.

SHIPS AND SETTLEMENT

The first European people to live in Australia settled close to the coast. The settlements of Sydney, Newcastle, Hobart, Launceston, Brisbane, Perth, Melbourne and Adelaide relied on sailing ships to bring people and supplies from Britain, and to provide communication links. Although sea journeys could take weeks or months, ships were the only transport between settlements in Australia, and between Australia and Britain. At that time there were no roads between the settlements, except some rough tracks linking neighbouring towns.

Steamships, such as the Oronsay, transported passengers and cargo until the 1960s when diesel power began to take over.

COLONIAL SHIPPING

Even after roads were built between settlements, sea travel remained the fastest and most reliable way to travel or send goods and messages. In those days, there were no telephones or radio. Sailing ships took messages as well as goods and passengers between the settlements and between Australia and Britain.

COASTAL TOWNS

Towns developed along the Australian coast at places where ships could find shelter from the wind and waves, and where they could get close to shore to unload goods. Towns were built at sheltered harbours such as Port Phillip (Melbourne), Port Jackson (Sydney) and King George Sound (Albany), and near river mouths such as the Derwent River (Hobart) and the Swan River (Perth).

STEAMSHIPS

From the 1850s, steamships began to take over from sailing ships. This made sea travel more reliable, faster and safer. Shipwrecks were less likely to happen, because steamships did not have to rely on wind to move away from danger.

Steamships greatly reduced the time taken for goods and people to travel between Britain and Australia. They also improved travel conditions between Australian towns and cities so messages could be received more quickly.

HOW A STEAMSHIP WORKS

In a steam engine, coal, or sometimes other types of fuel, is burned to heat water to turn it into steam. The steam takes up more space than the water, and pushes a piston that turns the propeller shaft. The turning propeller pushes water behind the ship, making the vessel move forwards.

PADDLE-STEAMERS

Paddle-steamers helped European farmers move into areas of inland eastern Australia. The Murray and Darling Rivers became the highways of the inland. Paddle-steamers transported wool from the sheep stations of inland Victoria and New South Wales to river ports, from where they were transported overland to Adelaide and Melbourne.

The first paddle-steamers started service in 1853 and carried gold diggers along the Murray River from Adelaide to the Victorian goldfields. They also brought supplies for inland towns and farms, and took bales of wool back to the city markets. Soon other paddle-steamers joined the river traffic, and services were extended along the Darling River to the northern parts of inland New South Wales.

Echuca: Paddle-steamers are no longer used to transport wool. Today, their cargo is tourists.

ECHUCA FOR SALE

Echuca was established in the 1850s by ex-convict Henry Hopwood, who built a punt across the Murray River there. He charged people to cross the river on his punt, and later built an inn on the southern bank. A small settlement grew around the inn, and soon wool, wheat and timber were being brought to Echuca on barges pulled by paddle-steamers. The goods were then taken overland to Melbourne for sale.

RIVER TOWNS

Towns including Echuca (Victoria) and Bourke (New South Wales) developed as river ports for paddle-steamers. Bourke was established at the point of navigation (the place where the river became too shallow for paddle-steamers to go further upstream). In northern Victoria, Echuca developed as a major inland port because it was the closest point on the Murray River to Melbourne. Goods were transported overland between Echuca and Melbourne by bullock dray, and after 1864, by rail.

Paddlesteamer 'Ellen' with bales of wool as part of her cargo

RAILWAYS TAKE OVER

River transport declined from the 1880s, as railways spread inland. Steam trains were faster than paddle-steamers, and goods could be transported to places other than river ports.

IMMIGRANT SHIPS

People have come to live in Australia from all over the world. Australia's first peoples, the Aboriginal peoples, travelled by boat to Australia's northern shores more than 50,000 years ago. After 1788, British immigrants started arriving aboard sailing ships. In 1851, gold discoveries encouraged thousands of hopeful diggers who arrived by sailing ship from all over the world, especially from the United States, China and Europe.

During the 1950s and 1960s, nearly three million people travelled to Australia aboard passenger liners

THE WRECK OF CATARAQUI

In 1845, the immigrant ship Cataraqui ran aground on King Island in Bass Strait. The sailing ship, carrying 367 immigrants and 44 crew from England bound for Melbourne, crashed into reef 150 metres from a rocky beach. Huge waves washed over the ship and many people drowned. After clinging to the remains of the wreck for a whole day, about 70 people tried to swim to safety. Only nine survived.

Cataraqui Shipwreck Site, King Island, 1887

AFTER WORLD WAR II

Between the end of World War II (1945) and 1970, nearly three million people were brought to Australia aboard large passenger ships. Many of the immigrants had been left homeless by the war in Europe. Immigrants travelled to Australia by ship until the 1970s when air travel became more affordable and passenger ships ceased to be the main form of international travel.

GREAT HARDSHIP

Conditions aboard immigrant ships were often harsh. There was no air-conditioning in the stuffy cabins below the waterline where most immigrants travelled. Water and food were rationed and the ships were badly overcrowded.

The 'New Australia' passenger liner bringing migrants to Australia

THE NEW AUSTRALIA

The New Australia brought about 40,000 migrants from England to Australia in 25 journeys between August 1950 and September 1957. It could carry about 1,600 passengers, who slept in six-berth cabins. It was built in 1931 as a luxury ocean liner. Then, in World War II, it was used as a troop ship. From 1957, it carried passengers between Europe and North America until it was scrapped in 1966.

EYEWITNESS ACCOUNT

One Polish immigrant, who arrived in Australia in 1950, described conditions aboard a migrant ship.

'There were 60 women and children to a room. The food was very bad and there was not enough fresh water so that on the Red Sea it was on only three times a day, one hour at a time. The heat and the shortage of water were driving us mad. Mothers were fanning their children who, although completely undressed were crying, gasping for air.'

PASSENGER SHIPS

CRUISE SHIPS

When aeroplanes became the most popular form of international travel in the 1960s and 1970s, many passenger liners were turned into cruise ships. Cruise ships are like travelling hotels, taking tourists on cruises to resorts and tourist destinations, such as islands in the South Pacific, including Fiji and Vanuatu.

Passengers aboard cruise ships sleep in cabins. Food is served in restaurants, and there are entertainment facilities such as swimming pools, cinemas, nightclubs and casinos.

PASSENGER FERRIES

In Sydney, ferries are an important form of public transport, carrying thousands of people every day. Ferries are also used in Brisbane, Perth and Hobart. They also operate between mainland Australia and islands - for example, between Fremantle and Rottnest Island in Western Australia, and between the mainland and islands such as Kangaroo Island (South Australia) and Flinders Island and King Island (Bass Strait).

CAR FERRIES

Passenger car ferries and other cargo ships are very important to Tasmania because goods cannot be transported there by road or rail.

Roll-on-roll-off car ferries carry cargo, and passengers and their cars. The cars are driven on to the ferry through a large door at either the bow or stern, and, at the end of the journey, are driven off the other end. Passengers travel on the upper decks.

FERRY TO TASMANIA

The Spirit of Tasmania is 194.3 metres long and weighs 28,000 tonnes. The Spirit of Tasmania is a roll-on-roll-off car ferry. It is the main ferry link between Tasmania and Melbourne. The Spirit of Australia I and II were constructed in Finland in 1998 and operated for four years between Greece and Italy. These two monohull vessels replaced the original MV Spirit of Tasmania, making their dual maiden voyages across Bass Strait on September 1, 2002.

Each ship can carry 1,400 passengers, 1,000 cars and has 750 berths. It travels between Melbourne and Devonport, taking between 9 and 11 hours.

CARGO SHIPS AND NAVAL SHIPS

Ships are used to transport freight, and are also used in Australia's defence force. There are different types of ships for different cargoes. The Royal Australian Navy has a fleet of ships to help provide Australia's defence.

CONTAINER VESSELS

General cargo is carried on large ships called container ships. The containers are large metal boxes, which can be carried by semi-trailer or train to the port. They can be packed before they are taken to the port for loading, which speeds up loading and unloading at the docks. Huge cranes are used to load the containers on the ships.

TANKERS

Liquids such as oil are carried in huge ships called tankers. In an oil tanker, the hull is divided into sections, each of which is filled with oil. Most tankers carry oil, although there are also tankers that carry other liquids such as petroleum, chemicals and wine.

LIVE ANIMAL CARRIERS

Live sheep and cattle are transported aboard specially-designed ships. The animals are kept in large pens below deck.

BULK CARRIERS

Solid, loose goods such as grain, iron ore and woodchips are carried in large ships called bulk carriers. They are loaded directly into the ships' holds, which have wide hatches to make loading and unloading easy.

NAVAL SHIPS

Naval ships are usually smaller and faster than cruise ships and cargo ships. Australia's naval fleet includes guided missile frigates and submarines. A fleet of small, fast patrol boats patrol Australia's coastline, and supply ships transport supplies for Australian armed forces overseas. The navy also has tankers for refuelling other naval ships at sea, as well as minesweepers, landing craft and tugs.

SHIPPING FOR TRADE

Australian goods are sold to other countries, and Australians buy goods made in other countries. Most of these goods are transported to and from Australia by ship.

Heavy goods and goods that take up large amounts of space are usually transported by ship. Only small, valuable items and goods that must be transported quickly to retain their freshness are transported by air. These may include gemstones such as diamonds, some types of seafood and cut flowers.

Goods, such as wheat and coal, are loaded loose (unpacked) directly to and from the holds of bulk carriers.

TRANSPORTING EXPORTS

Most of Australia's trade is with countries in Asia and Europe. Iron ore and coal are shipped to Japan and South Korea aboard huge bulk carriers, which are loaded at ports on the coast of Western Australia, Queensland and New South Wales. Bauxite and alumina (which are used to make aluminium) are also shipped to Japan and other Asian countries from Weipa and Gladstone (Queensland), Kwinana and Sunbury (Western Australia) and Gove (Northern Territory). Live sheep are shipped to the Middle East, and wine is transported aboard container ships to Asia, Europe and North America.

INTERSTATE TRADE

Australian goods may be transported to other states by ship, although rail and road transport are more commonly used. Ships are used to transport iron ore from South Australia and Western Australia to steelworks in New South Wales. Bauxite from the Northern Territory and Queensland is transported by ship to aluminium smelters in New South Wales and Tasmania. Oil and petrol are also shipped between states.

IMPORTS AND EXPORTS

Imports are goods that are brought into a country. Most of Australia's imports are manufactured goods such as machinery, electrical goods, processed foods, and motor vehicles.

Exports are goods that are sold to buyers in other countries. Australia's main exports are agricultural and mining products, although the export of manufactured goods such as motor vehicles, machinery, and processed foods is increasing.

Forklift is handling and stacking sugar bags in hold of bulk-vessel

RO-RO

PORTS AND HARBOURS

Ships berth at more than 70 Australian ports. Ports in Australia are controlled by port corporations, which are set up by State Governments, and employ over 33,700 people. Port corporations control the movement of ships within the port and provide loading and unloading facilities. They charge shipping companies to use the ports.

Cranes are used to load and unload ships at container terminals

FAST FACT

More than 90% of the world trade is covered by sea

Large ships are difficult to manoeuvre. Tugs are used to move them within the harbour.

BERTHING

The harbourmaster (the person in charge of the port) decides which berth an incoming ship will be given. The berth depends on the type of ship. For example, a bulk coal carrier would be berthed at the coal loader, and a container ship would be berthed at a container terminal. Ships wait outside the port until a berth is available.

TUGS

In busy ports, tugs are used to manoeuvre large ships. Tugs are small boats with powerful engines. They pull large ships away from their berths, and guide them along the channels in the port until it is safe for the ship to go on unassisted.

LOADING AND UNLOADING

Different types of cargo need different types of berths. Ports such as Dampier in Western Australia have conveyor belts to load huge amounts of iron ore on to bulk carriers. Newcastle Harbour has special berths for loading coal and wheat. Container ships are berthed at container terminals, where large cranes transfer containers between the ships and trains or semi-trailers. Cars are transported aboard special ships designed so the cars can be driven on and off at the wharf.

CUSTOMS AND QUARANTINE

Goods and passengers from other countries must pass through customs at ports. Some goods, especially plants and animals, have to be kept separate for a period of time to make sure they are not carrying diseases or pests. This is called quarantining. In most cases, quarantined goods and animals are taken to a secure area away from the port.

SAFETY AT SEA

The safety of sea transport has improved greatly in the last 100 years. Ships today use satellite navigation. This tells a captain the ship's exact position and is used to check the positions of other ships to avoid collisions. If a ship does get into trouble, radio and satellite communications enable help to be sent quickly. Radio beacons can send out continuous signals to help search and rescue vessels to find survivors quickly. Modern maps and charts are also more accurate, and ships are fitted with better life rafts than ships of the past.

SAFETY ORGANISATIONS

Shipping safety in Australia is controlled by the Australian Maritime Safety Authority (AMSA), which is run by the Federal Government. It keeps records of all ships in Australian waters, and makes sure that they are seaworthy. AMSA also coordinates search and rescue operations. Port authorities are responsible for safety within their ports.

ENTERING AND LEAVING PORT

Ship movements are watched from a central point in the port, which in large ports is a control tower. There are navigational and safety aids to help prevent accidents as ships enter and leave ports. Wave rider buoys at the port entrance measure the height of the swell. If the swell is too large, ships are not allowed to enter or leave the port. Wind measurement is also important as strong winds can blow large ships off course.

The harbour pilot and tugs help to ensure ships do not run aground or collide with other ships. The pilot has knowledge of local conditions, and tugs are used to help ships manoeuvre through narrow channels. Channels within the port are marked by buoys and markers called leads, which the pilot uses to help keep the ship in the middle of the channel.

PORT PHILLIP BAY

To get to the port of Melbourne, ships enter Port Phillip Bay through a narrow entrance called The Rip. The Rip is one of the most treacherous stretches of water in the world, and great skill is required to bring ships through safely. Pilots specially trained in handling The Rip's conditions board ships outside the entrance, and guide them through The Rip and through Port Phillip Bay to Port Melbourne. The dangerous waters have claimed the lives of many seamen over the years, including some pilots who have fallen overboard while boarding or leaving vessels in rough seas. The Rip pilot service has operated since 1838, and today employs 32 pilots.

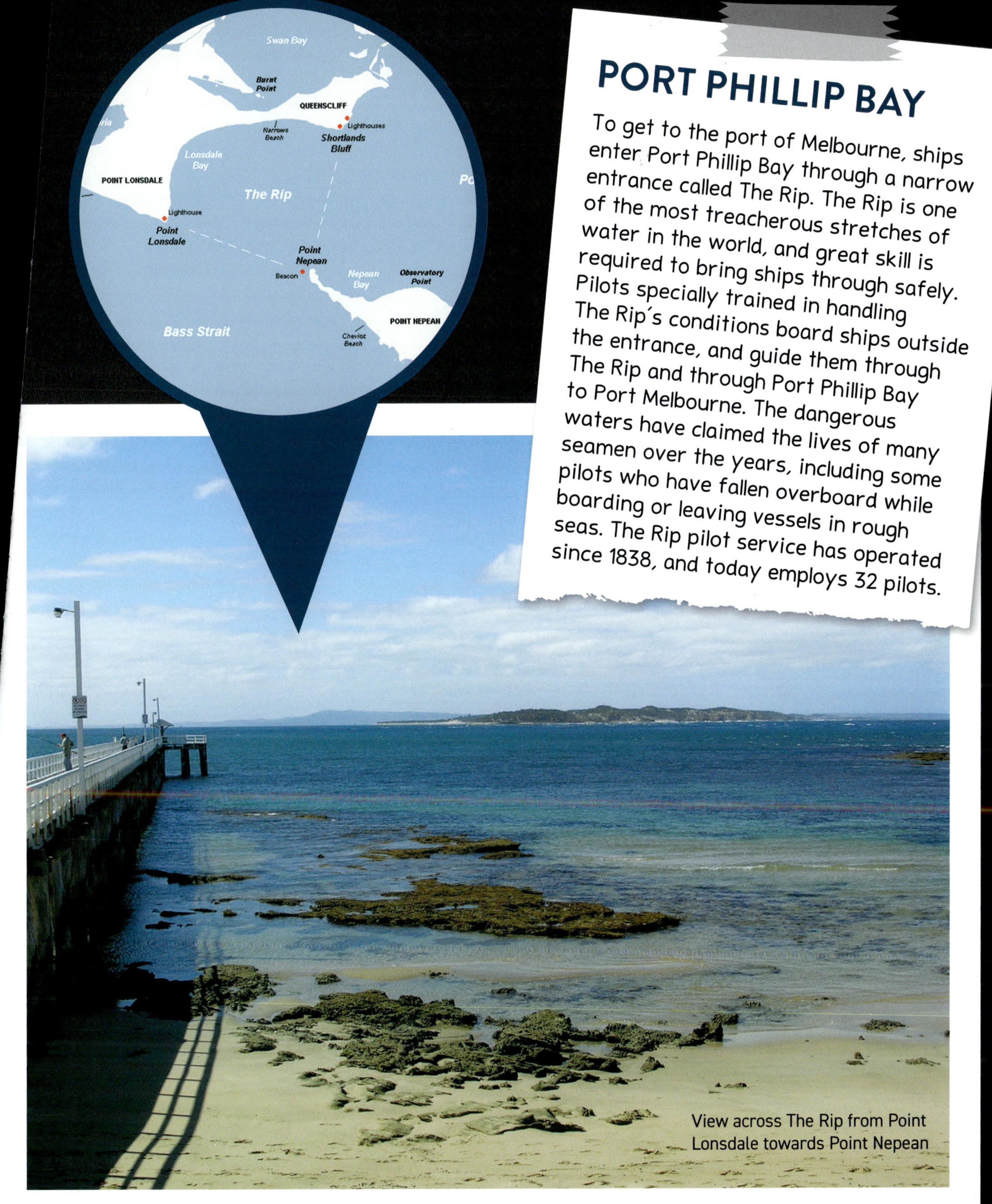

View across The Rip from Point Lonsdale towards Point Nepean

SEARCH AND RESCUE

Even with modern safety standards, sea vessels sometimes need help. Search and rescue operations search for missing craft, help vessels in distress and rescue crews of boats in trouble.

MARITIME RESCUE COORDINATION CENTRE

In Australia, search and rescue operations are organised by the Maritime Rescue Coordination Centre, which is a part of the Australian Maritime Safety Authority (AMSA). If a ship is in difficulty, it sends an emergency distress signal, which is picked up by a Coast Radio Station (CRS). These stations are found in Sydney, Brisbane, Melbourne, Perth, Darwin and Townsville, and are operated by AMSA.

SAFETY PROBLEMS IN THE PAST

Ships today are much safer than ships of the past. Many shipwrecks occurred when strong winds blew sailing ships on to land or reefs. Other ships were wrecked because there was not enough wind to control the ship's direction, and waves or currents pushed them into dangerous positions. The development of steamships made shipwrecks less common. Steamships did not rely on the wind to move, and they could move out of danger more easily.

Shipwrecks on Moreton Island, Queensland

RESCUE TEAMS

Many coastal towns and ports have small volunteer rescue teams that work to help ships in distress in their local area. Major rescues may also involve private organisations such as helicopter and aeroplane operators, and the navy may also be used. Aircraft can locate ships and survivors quickly, especially if distress beacons are used to guide searchers to the scene. Helicopters, rescue launches and aeroplanes can all be used in search and rescue operations.

AUSTRALIA'S SEARCH AND RESCUE REGION

Australia is responsible for search and rescue in the eastern half of the Indian Ocean, the south west Pacific Ocean and the Southern Ocean. The area covers nearly 53 million square kilometres, making up more than 10% of the Earth's surface.

The Rescue of Apostle Andrew

In 1997, a Russian training ship called Apostle Andrew lost its rudder 2,900 kilometres south-east of Perth. It was wallowing out of control in 20-metre swell. An amateur radio operator picked up the distress signal, and notified the Maritime Rescue Coordination Centre. They radioed an Australian fishing vessel in the area, asking it to assist the Russian ship. The Australian crew helped the Russian sailors make an emergency rudder, and the Apostle Andrew travelled on to Fremantle to be repaired.

SHIPPING AND THE ENVIRONMENT

BALLAST WATER

When bulk carriers and tankers are empty or carrying small loads, they carry ballast water to keep the ship stable in the water. This may cause pollution when the water is discharged (pumped out), as it may contain oil or other pollutants from where the ship originally pumped the water aboard. Ballast water may also contain seaweed or sea creatures from other parts of the world, such as the Pacific seastar (a kind of starfish). These plants and animals can become pests in Australian waters. The Pacific seastar now lives in the estuary of the Derwent River in Tasmania. It was probably introduced to the river in ballast water from Japan in the 1980s. Up to 30 million of the starfish live on the riverbed eating vast amounts of sea grasses, small sea creatures and fish eggs, causing great problems for the river ecosystem.

Sometimes ships' crews use sea water to clean tanks, which can also cause pollution when the water is pumped back into the ocean.

A tanker spilling its supply of ballast water at dock

OIL SPILLS

Oil spills can cause serious damage to the environment. Oil can be spilt from oil tankers if they collide or run aground. Fuel leaking from sunken vessels can also cause water pollution. Oil and fuel spills can devastate coastlines and cause the death of seabirds, fish and water plants.

LAURA D'AMATO OIL SPILL

On the night of August 3, 1999, the Italian oil tanker Laura D'Amato was unloading its cargo at an oil depot in Sydney Harbour. A mistake caused 250 tonnes of oil to be pumped directly into the harbour. Booms (long floating barriers) were put up around the spill, but some oil leaked out and spread to other parts of the harbour, covering the shoreline with a layer of oil.

Helicopters were used to track the oil and direct oil-removal boats that scooped the oil from the surface of the water. More than 300 people were involved in the clean-up, including experts from Queensland, Victoria and New Zealand. The shipping company and the ship's captain were fined as a result of the spill.

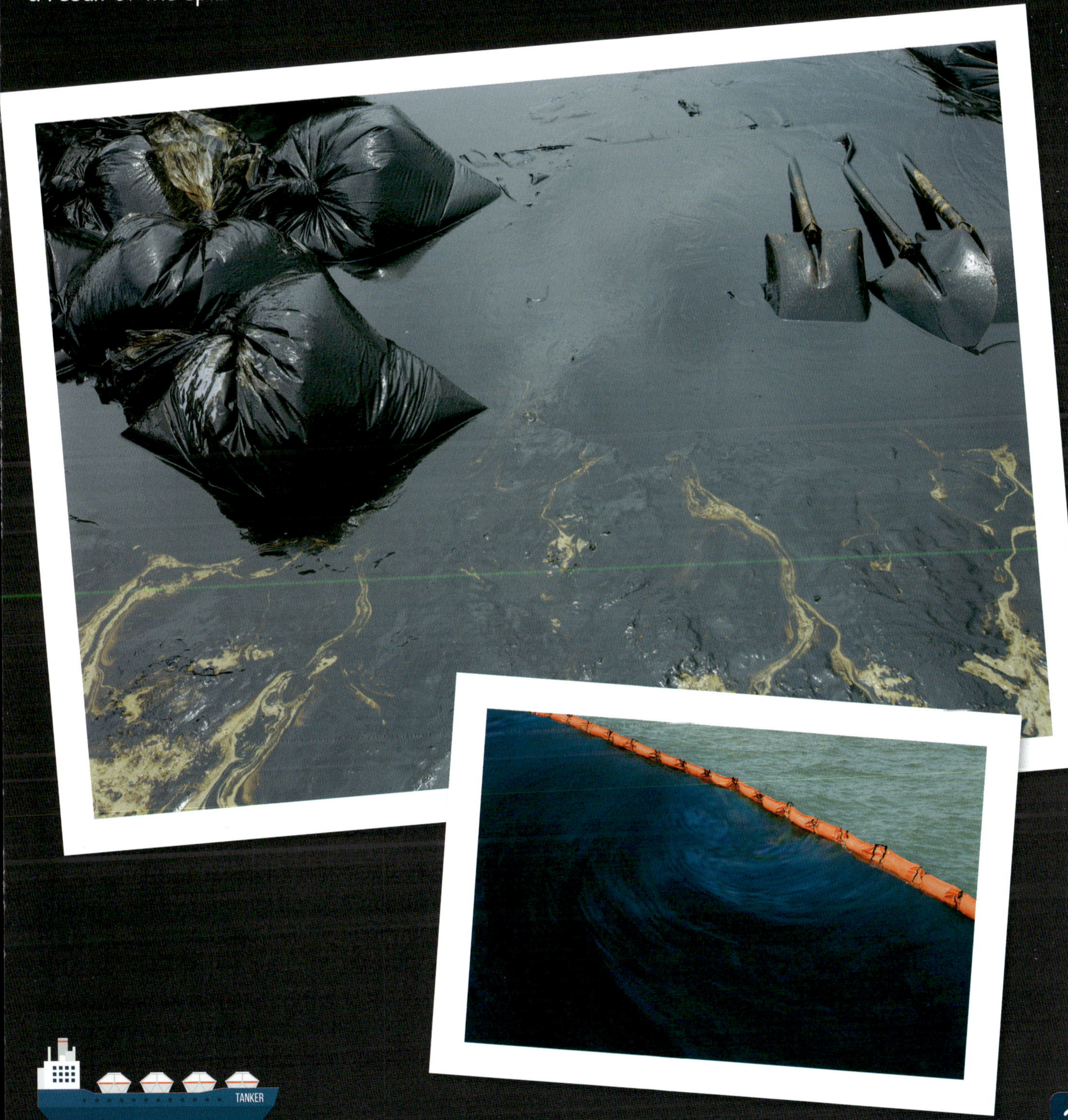

TANKER

WORKING IN THE SHIPPING INDUSTRY

The shipping industry employs people on ships and on shore. People who work on ships spend long periods away from home.

Navigation officer manages devices, looking ahead on the navigation bridge of ocean ship

JOBS ON SHORE

Many people are employed to operate Australian ports.

JOBS ON SHIPS

Many ships visiting Australian ports are owned by overseas companies, and their crews come from many different nations. Australian-owned ships usually employ Australian crews.

The captain (also called the master) is in charge of the ship. Officers who are experts in navigation, communications and engineering help the captain. Other workers on ships include mechanics, deckhands and cooks.

Pilots control ships as they enter and leave port. Pilots are experienced in local conditions and keep ships within the harbour channels. Pilots also direct the operations of the tugs. The pilot is taken to the ship in a powerful pilot launch, and usually takes the wheel of the ship while it is in the port.

Seaway control tower on the Gold Coast

HARBOURMASTERS

The harbourmaster is in charge of the port, making sure ships enter and leave the port safely. Most harbourmasters were once ships' captains. The signal master communicates with ships waiting to enter and leave the port, and watches all shipping movements from a control tower.

Messages between the harbourmaster and the pilot are passed through the signal master. Ships contact the signal station as they approach the port, and receive advice on the best place to anchor as they wait for a berth in the port.

CUSTOMS AND IMMIGRATION OFFICIALS

Customs officers are government officials who inspect goods coming into the country, and collect tariffs. Tariffs are taxes paid on certain goods brought into the country. Customs officers also search for illegal goods such as weapons and drugs. Passengers and crew have their passports checked by immigration officials.

Quarantine officers check that goods coming into the country do not carry diseases or pests.

STEVEDORES

Stevedores supervise teams of workers, including fork-lift drivers and crane operators, in unloading and loading ships.

FIND OUT MORE

PRIMARY AND SECONDARY SOURCES

A primary source is information created by someone who was a part of or witnessed the historical event first hand. Primary sources are very important to historians researching events and time periods. Examples of primary sources are letters, emails, filmed interviews and clips, journals and diaries, census statistics, government documents, art and maps (from the time period), the news (both print and film), photographs and maps.

A secondary source is when someone who did not actually witness the event retells the facts that someone else told them. Examples of secondary sources include news (both print and film), interviews, letters, journals and diaries, biographies, textbooks and paraphrased quotations.

SEARCH KEY WORDS

Ships
Spirit of Australia
harbourmaster
Ports Australia
shipping routes

PRIMARY AND SECONDARY SOURCES SEARCH

The Sea Shepherd conservation group says it has caught the Japanese whaling ship Nisshin Maru in Australian waters with a slaughtered whale. Sea Shepherd's ship often tracks Japanese whaling ships in Australian waters.

Can you find some primary and secondary sources for this event?

GLOSSARY

berth a place where a ship is tied up; to dock a ship in its berth

bow the front of a ship

buoy a floating marker showing the edge of a channel or a hazardous spot

exports goods that are sold overseas

fleet a large group of ships organised by the one company (the navy)

frigate a small fast warship

harbour a large, sheltered bay suitable for ships to dock in

imports goods that are brought into the nation

landing craft a naval vessel that takes troops from ships to shore. Landing craft are designed to come close enough to the beach for troops to wade ashore.

manoeuvre skilfully move within a small space

mine sweeper a naval vessel that detects and destroys mines (floating bombs)

navigation directing the course of a ship (or other vehicle)

outrigger canoe canoe with a second smaller hull to help make the canoe stable

paddle-steamer a river boat with paddles on large wheels that are turned using steam power, making the boat move through the water

point of navigation the place where a river becomes too shallow for ships to travel further upstream

port a place where ships are loaded and unloaded

punt a shallow-bottomed boat used to transport passengers and goods across rivers

satellite an object in space that moves around a larger object. Communications satellites move around the Earth. They receive signals from one part of the Earth's surface and send them to another part of the Earth's surface.

stern the rear part of a ship

swell the movement of water in waves

tug a small boat with a powerful motor used to manoeuvre large ships in harbours

wave rider buoys buoys that measure the height of swells

wharf a platform built in a port for ships to berth at

INDEX